Mouth₁
Recip

MW01292736

Muffin Tin Recipes

55 Perfectly Portioned Muffin Tin Meals For Breakfast, Lunch, Dinner, Or After School Snacks!

Sarah Brooks

STOP!!! Before you read any further....Would you like to know the secrets of Anti-Aging?

If your answer is yes, then you are not alone. Thousands of people are looking for the secret to reducing wrinkles, looking younger, and maintaining a youthful appearance.

If you have been searching for these answers without much luck, you are in the right place!

Not only will you gain incredible insight in this book, but because I want to make sure to give you as much value as possible, right now for a limited time you can get full **100% FREE access to a VIP bonus EBook** entitled **Anti-Aging Made Easy!**

Just Go Here For Free Instant Access:

www.LuxyLifeNaturals.com

.

Legal Notice

Disclaimer Notice

Table Of Contents

Introduction

Not everyone is a gifted cook, nor a gifted baker. That doesn't mean though that those who are not gifted with culinary abilities should be resigned to sit in the sidelines all the time and let other people shine in the cooking and baking department. Many of us might just have limited time to spend in the kitchen, for example. Surely, many of us also just lack practice.

It is always best to start small if you have limited to zero knowledge in any field. As for cooking and baking, it's best to start with simple recipes and small servings.

What better way to start then than to practice with muffin tin meals? And if you're simply looking for easy-to-prepare, quick-cook meals, this book will definitely be a big help to you!

I want to thank you and congratulate you for purchasing the book *Muffin Tin Recipes: Mouthwatering Muffin Tin Recipes In 20 minutes!*

This book contains 55 recipes for muffin tin meals that you can cook for 20 minutes or less. These are tried and tested home recipes that have been handed down from generation to generation.

Experience the relaxing and fulfilling joy of cooking and baking muffin tin recipes! Impress your family, friends, or even co-workers with your culinary magic as you serve them with these delicious meals and treats. No need to think about what to serve for breakfast, lunch or dinner; you'll get plenty of ideas here. Give your kids incentive to come home early from school or sports practice with the delicious snack recipes that are sure to tickle their taste buds!

Thanks again for purchasing this book, I hope you enjoy it!

Chapter 1: Basic Instructions For Muffin Tin Meals

The rule of thumb for baking and cooking muffin tin meals is this: follow the instructions in the recipes, but be prepared to experiment with various ingredients.

What's great about these small servings is that you can easily manipulate how the dishes will end up. Since each serving is set separately, you are at liberty to experiment with just one or two of the muffins. After all, even if they don't turn out so well, the rest of the batch will still be good to serve.

A careful switch of the ingredients may produce a whole new flavor! Of course, one cannot simply change ingredients without careful thought. That leaves you with the toppings, but even changing just that can be very fun already.

Just have fun with these recipes and see how easily you can prepare them! Most importantly, enjoy the delicious meals and snacks you're going to make

Chapter 2: Why Muffin Tin Meals

There are so many reasons that it is a great idea to cook muffin tin meals! For starters, they are quick to prepare and easy to do. Even if you are not an experienced cook, you can definitely whip something up with the help of this recipe book.

Another good thing about muffin tin meals is that they are served in single portions. So even if you double the recipe, the servings will be cooked in single portions. Some of the recipes here can be kept frozen overnight, so you can set aside some for the next day, or for other people if you wish to share!

Serving muffin tin meals during parties can also help control everyone's food consumption. Single servings reinforce the idea that you don't need to have too much on your plate to appreciate the dish. Guests will be encouraged to put just enough food on their plates, and are therefore less likely to waste food. Should there be any leftovers, it will be very easy to store them or wrap them up to be given away

Chapter 3: Materials & Tools: What You Will Need To Get Started

Each recipe for any dish will require different kinds of tools and materials. There are similar tools, however, and there is one particular item that will be needed for all recipes in this book: A muffin tin. You may use a 6-cup tray, or 9 or 12—any of these will do. You just need to estimate how many cups each recipe can fill.

It is important to have a muffin tin that is made from high quality steel. In Chapter 9, there is a reminder that it is not a great idea to purchase a cheap muffin tin without closely examining the thickness of the material used. A non-stick muffin tin is a great option, but it's not exactly a requirement. A rubber version isn't advisable because these meals and snacks are to be baked at high temperatures. Even if the manufacturer claim the tray to be heat-resistant, it is best to simply avoid the possibility of ingesting toxins due to rubber reacting to heat.

Other materials and tools that will be needed throughout this book are:

> -Cooking spray
> -Olive oil (alternative to cooking spray)
> -Oven
> -Electric mixer
> -Assortment of bowls
> -Measuring cups and spoons
> -Refrigerator/freezer

Chapter 4: Muffin Tin Recipes For Breakfast

These recipes are very easy to do. Most importantly, it takes only a few minutes to put them all together. That's a relief for when you're in a hurry in the morning and can't spare more than 30 minutes just preparing breakfast!

1. Egg and Bacon Cups

Ingredients:

- 16 slices of bacon

- 8 eggs

- 1 can Pillsbury Grands! Homestyle Buttermilk Biscuits refrigerated dough

Steps:

- Preheat oven to 350° F.

- Cook the bacon strips in a pan, but not thoroughly enough that the edges are crispy.

- In a non-stick muffin tray, fill ¾ of each cup with the dough. Press some up to the sides to make the biscuit "cups".

- Add two bacon strips and crack an egg in each cup.

- Bake egg and bacon muffin cups for 20 minutes. Serve warm.

2. Mini Sausage Pies

Ingredients:

- 3/4 lbs. ground pork sausage

- 1/2 cup chopped onion

- 1/2 tsp salt

- 1 cup sliced mushrooms

- 3 tbsp. chopped sage

- 1 cup Cheddar cheese

- 2 eggs

- 1/2 cup milk

- 1/2 cup Original Bisquick mix

Steps:

- Preheat oven to 375° F.

- Use a skillet to cook the sausage and onion over medium heat. Constantly stir for 5 minutes until the meat starts to brown. Drain and let cool.

- Add salt, sage, mushrooms and cheese. Stir and set aside.

- In a large bowl, whisk the eggs, milk and Bisquick mix.

- In a non-stick muffin pan, place one tablespoon of the baking mix in each cup.

- Add in the sausage mix.

- Cover with another tablespoon of the baking mix.

- Bake for 20 minutes until the tops turn golden brown.

3. Cheesy Broccoli and Ham Muffins

Ingredients:

- 2 cups sliced broccoli

- 1/2 cup cooked ham (sliced and diced)

- 1 1/2 cup muffin mix

- 1/2 cup milk

- 1 egg

- 3 tbsp. vegetable oil

- 1/2 cup Cheddar cheese

- choice spices and seasoning (garlic, onions, salt, pepper, etc...)

Steps:

- Preheat oven to 400° F.

- Toss the broccoli in a pan and season according to taste. You can add garlic, onions, some salt and pepper. Just make sure the broccoli don't turn soggy.

- In a large bowl, combine the muffin mix, milk, egg and vegetable oil.

- Add the cooked broccoli, ham and Cheddar cheese. Mix well.

- Spritz a muffin tin with cooking spray and spoon the mixture in each cup.

- Bake for 20minutes until the tops are golden brown.

4. Baked Oatmeal

Ingredients:

- 1 cup steel cut oats

- 1/2 cup raisins

- 1/3 cup chopped walnuts or almonds

- 1/2 tsp. nutmeg

- 1 tsp. cinnamon

- 1/4 tsp. salt

- 2 eggs

- 1/4 cup peanut butter

- 1 1/2 cup milk

- 1/3 cup maple syrup

- 1 apple (chopped in small cubes)

- maple syrup

Steps:

- Soak the oats in a bowl of water and leave overnight.

- Preheat the oven to 375° F.

- Drain the oats and transfer in a large mixing bowl. Add the raisins, nuts, half a teaspoon of the cinnamon, and salt.

- In another bowl, lightly beat the eggs and then whisk in the butter and milk.

- Add the oats and nuts mixture and stir until all ingredients are well-combined.

- Spoon the oats into the muffin tin.

- Take another bowl and toss in the chopped apples with what's left of the cinnamon. Use this to top the oats in each cup.

- Bake for 20 minutes.

- Serve with a drizzle of maple syrup.

5. Pancakes Puffs and Fruit

Ingredients:

- 1 cup flour

- 1 cup milk

- 6 eggs

- 1/4 cup melted butter

- 1 pinch of salt

- sliced fresh strawberries, blueberries or bananas (you can also use jam)

- maple or sugar syrup

Steps:

- Preheat oven to 400° F.

- In a large bowl, mix all the ingredients until smooth. You may also use a handheld mixer or even blender.

- Grease or use a cooking spray on the muffin pan.

- Pour the pancake mixture evenly in the cups. Filling them halfway through will suffice.

- Bake for 15 minutes or until the pancakes turn puffy and golden brown.

- Once cooked, use a knife or fork to pop off the pancake puffs.

- When the pancakes start to cool, the center portion will flatten and slightly form a cup. Take your sliced fruit and spoon them in top of the pancakes.

- Drizzle with syrup and serve.

6. Hash Browns

Ingredients:

- 1 bag Simply Potatoes Shredded Hash Browns

- (optional: Take 6 russet potatoes, peel, shred, and rinse off. Use paper towels to absorb more of the water.)

- 1/2 cup chopped onion springs

- 2 tsp. black pepper

- 1 tsp. kosher salt

- 3 tbsp. olive oil

- 1/2 cup parmesan cheese

- butter

Steps:

- Preheat oven from 400° to 450° F.

- Place the shredded potatoes in a bowl. Add in the onions, olive oil, and season with salt and pepper. You may add other seasonings if you wish. Toss with a fork until well mixed.

- Take a muffin tin and grease with butter. (In lieu of butter, you may also use cooking spray.)

- Spoon the potatoes in each cup. Pack in the potatoes gently using the back of a spoon.

- Slow bake for an hour or until you can see that the sides have turned crispy brown.

- Let cool for about ten minutes. Remove carefully with a fork.

- Flip the hash browns so that the crispy bottom and sides are visible. Serve warm.

7. Scrambled Eggs in Cups

Ingredients:

- 2 cups pancake mix

- 8 eggs

- 3/4 cup milk

- 1/3 cup Cheddar cheese

- 1/2 cup cheese sauce

- 1/8 tsp. pepper

- 1 tbsp. butter

- 3 tbsps. cooked bacon bits

- 1 tbsp. chopped chives

Steps:

- Preheat oven to 425° F.

- In a bowl, mix the pancake mix, cheese and ½ cup milk.

- Take out the dough and knead. Shape it into a 10-inch roll.

- Cut the roll in 12. Place each piece in a cup and press along the bottom and sides, up to the rim.

- Bake for 10 minutes. Press the crust with a spoon if they turn fluffy once taken out of the oven.

- In another bowl, beat the eggs with the remaining milk. Add pepper.

- In a skillet, melt the butter and add the egg mixture. Stir for several minutes. Fold in the pasta sauce and bacon bits until you have a moist, scrambled egg mixture.

- Remove the baked cups first before spooning in the scrambled eggs. Serve with chives and more bacon bits on top.

8. Eggs Benedict in Cups

Ingredients:

- 1 pack hollandaise sauce mix

- 1 can Pillsbury Grands! Refrigerated buttermilk biscuits dough

- 6 oz. sliced bacon or ham

- 8 eggs (cold)

- 1 large tomato

- 2 tsps. chopped chives

- salt

- pepper

Steps:

- Preheat oven to 350° F.

- Prepare hollandaise sauce as instructed.

- Use cooking spray on the muffin tin.

- Cut the dough into eight equal parts. Press each piece at the bottom and up the sides of the cups to form the crust.

- Place some bacon pieces in each cup

- Add one teaspoon hollandaise sauce.

- Slice the tomato thinly and add one on top of each cup. Top with another teaspoon of Hollandaise sauce.

- Bake for 20 minutes until golden brown. Let cool and remove from the muffin tin.

- Use a skillet to boil 3 inches of water.

- Break an egg into a small glass bowl and hold close to the water. Slowly slide the egg into the water. Let it cook for about three minutes until the yolk is firm. Remove with a draining spoon. Repeat with the rest of the eggs.

- Place each egg carefully in each cup. Drizzle half a teaspoon hollandaise sauce on top, then sprinkle chives, salt and pepper.

9. Baked Eggs

Ingredients:

- 1 pack sliced deli ham

- 4 large tomatoes

- 1 cup cheddar cheese

- small eggs

- salt

- pepper

Steps:

Preheat the oven to 350° F.

Use non-stick spray on the muffin tin.

Place one slice of ham at the bottom of each cup.

Chop the tomatoes and add scoop in a teaspoon each.

Sprinkle cheddar cheese on top.

Gently break a small egg in each cup, making sure that the yolk doesn't break.

Sprinkle a little salt and pepper on top.

Bake for 20 minutes until the egg whites are cooked and the yolks a little firm.

10. Artichoke & Spinach Bites

Ingredients:

- 4 oz. cream cheese (chilled)

- 10 oz. frozen spinach (thawed and drained)

- 2 cans artichokes

- 1 cup milk

- 1 1/2 cups biscuit mix

- 1 cup grated parmigiano-reggiano cheese

Steps:

- Preheat oven to 350° F.

- Drain the artichokes and chop.

- Chop cream cheese into small cubes.

- In a bowl, mix artichokes, biscuit mix, milk and cheese. Fold in the cream cheese cubes.

- Use cooking spray on muffin tin.

- Spoon the mixture in each cup then bake for 15 minutes.

11. Burger Cups

Ingredients:

- 1 1/2 lb. ground lean beef

- 4 oz. cream cheese

- 1 can Pillsbury Grands! Refrigerated biscuits dough

- 1 egg

- 1 tsp. water

- 1/2 cup ketchup

- 1/3 cup pickle relish

- 2 tbsps. yellow mustard

- 2 tbsps. sesame seeds

- 1 tsp. onion powder

- 1/2 tsp. salt

- 1/2 tsp. black pepper

Steps:

- Preheat oven at 350° F.

- Cook beef over medium heat until half cooked. Drain and add cream cheese, ketchup, pickle relish, onion powder, salt and pepper. Cook until mixture is creamy.

- Slice the biscuit doughs in half.

- Grease the muffin tin.

- Press half of the dough at the bottom of each cup and halfway up the sides.

- Spoon the cooked beef evenly in each cup, then cover with the other halves of the dough.

- In a bowl, beat the egg and water, and glaze on top of the dough.

- Sprinkle sesame seeds on top.

- Bake for 15-20 minutes.

12. Shepherd's Pie

Ingredients:

- 1 lb. ground meat

- 4 oz. cream cheese

- 1 cup mixed vegetables

- 1 cup mashed potatoes

- 1/2 cup gravy

- 1/4 cup cheddar cheese

- 2 cloves garlic (crushed)

Steps:

- Cook the meat and season to taste. Let cool a little.

- Preheat oven at 375° F.

- Mix mashed potatoes with cream cheese, cheddar and garlic.

- Add vegetables and gravy to the meat.

- Spoon the meat mixture in each muffin tin cup. Cover with the mashed potatoes and sprinkle with more cheese.

- Bake for 20 minutes.

13. Chicken Enchilada

Ingredients:

- tortilla shells dough

- chicken

- 1/2 can black beans

- 1 medium bell pepper (chopped)

- 1/2 cup chopped onions

- 1/2 cup shredded cheese

- 1/2 cup diced jalapenos

- 1/2 cup crumbled goat cheese

- 4 tbsps. enchilada sauce

Steps:

- Preheat oven at 400° F.

- Add all ingredients in a large bowl and mix well.

- Cut up the tortilla shells in smaller circles, depending on how big your muffin tin is.

- Grease the muffin tin.

- Press one tortilla dough in each cup.

- Add one teaspoon of the enchilada mixture, and cover with another tortilla dough. Repeat until the cups are full.

- Bake for 15 minutes.

14. Caesar Salad in Crouton Cups

Ingredients:

- 12 white bread (pressed until firm and thin)

- 3 cups Romaine lettuce

- 1/4 cup Caesar salad dressing

- 1/4 cup grated parmesan

- 3 tbsps. unsalted butter

- 1 tbsp. dried thyme

- 1 tbsp. dried parsley

- 2 tsps. garlic powder

- black pepper

Steps:

- Preheat oven to 375° F.

- Remove the crusts of the sliced bread to have 4-inch squares.

- Lightly butter both sides.

- Press a piece of bread inside each cup. Allow the corners to stick up.

- Bake for 12 minutes, then remove the bread shells and let cool.

- In a bowl, mix the lettuce and Caesar dressing.

- Spoon salad into the bread cups. Sprinkle cheese on top and serve.

Chapter 5: Muffin Tin Recipes For Lunch

Lunch meals are ideally heavy and filling. Most of us eat a little breakfast because of busy schedules. This is why when it comes to our midday repast, we need something more filling and nourishing to get us through the rest of the day. Even those who only have time for a sandwich run would want to make sure that they get the good stuff in: greens, veggies, sometimes fruit, and meat cuts.

Here are some muffin tin recipes that you can make at home, or prepare the day before and bring to work for lunch.

15. Cheesy Sweet Potato Muffins

Ingredients:

- 2 medium-sized sweet potatoes

- 2 eggs

- 1 tbsp. olive oil

- 1/3 cup melted butter

- 1/2 cup milk

- 1 1/2 cups all-purpose flour

- 1 1/2 cups baby spinach, kale, or other greens of choice

- 1 pinch salt

- 1 pinch ground black pepper

- 2 tsp. baking powder

- 2 tsp. brown sugar (packed)

- 3/4 cup feta cheese (crumbled)

- 1/2 cup Gruyère cheese (shredded)

Steps:

- Peel the potatoes and cut into chunky cubes about half an inch big.

- Coarsely chop the kale or spinach or your choice of greens.

- Preheat the oven to 400° F.

- In a non-stick pan, toss the sweet potatoes in olive oil.

- Pour the potatoes in a baking pan and bake for 20-25 minutes. Stir the contents of the pan after 10 minutes to help it cook evenly.

- Once the potatoes are tender, remove from the oven and let cool.

- Beat the eggs in a big bowl. Add the melted butter and milk, and whisk to blend.

- Slowly add the flour, brown sugar, salt, pepper and baking powder. Using a spoon or spatula, stir just enough to moisten the dry ingredients.

- Add the baked sweet potatoes.

- Add the kale and cheeses, then mix.

- Take a regular-sized muffin tin and spritz with non-stick cooking spray.

- Fill up to 3/4 of each cup with the potato batter.

- Bake from 18-22 minutes.

16. Beef-Barbecue Mini Pies

Ingredients:

- 1 lb. lean, ground beef

- 1/3 cup barbecue sauce (may be canned or your personal recipe)

- 1/2 cup chopped onions

- 1/2 cup chopped bell pepper

- 1 1/2 cup Cheddar cheese

- 2 eggs

- 1 cup milk

- 1 cup choice muffin mix

- liquid shortening

Steps:

- Preheat oven to 400° F.

- In a skillet, cook the beef over medium heat. Add the chopped bell pepper and onions. Stir occasionally until brown.

- Drain the beef and transfer to a mixing bowl. Pour in the barbecue sauce and mix.

- Take the muffin tin and grease with liquid shortening.

- Spoon in the beef and fill about 3/4 of each cup.

- Sprinkle three-quarters of the cheese on top of the beef.

- In another bowl, whisk the eggs, milk and muffin mix until well blended.

- Pour a bit of the mix in each cup without letting it overflow.

- Bake for 25 minutes.

- Sprinkle the remaining cheese over the steaming muffins. You can bake it again for 5 extra minutes or until the cheese melts completely.

17. Crab Cakes

Ingredients:

- 6 ounces fresh crab meat (shredded)

- 1 cup cream cheese (separate in 1/4 cup and 3/4 cup)

- 1 cup parmesan cheese

- 1 1/2 cups panko (or fine bread crumbs without the crust)

- 1 egg

- 1 lemon (you just need it for the zest)

- 4 tsps. Chopped chives

- 1 stick melted butter

- 1/4 tsp. salt

- cheyenne pepper

Steps:

- Preheat the oven to 350° F.

- In a large bowl, beat the cream cheese using a handheld mixer to smoothen the texture.

- Add a fourth of the parmesan cheese, egg and seasoning.

- Rub the lemon on a fine metal shredder. Let the zest fall directly into the bowl.

- Add the crab meat and fold all ingredients together.

- In another bowl, toss in the panko, the remaining 3/4 cup parmesan cheese, and chives.

- Pour the melted butter and toss again with a fork until well-mixed with the dry ingredients.

- Grease or spritz a muffin tin with cooking spray.

- Press one tablespoon of the panko mixture in each cup. Using your thumbs, create a crust at the bottom and up the sides.

- Fill the cups with another teaspoon of the crab meat mixture. Loosely top with some more panko.

- Bake for 20 minutes.

18. Chicken or Beef Tacos

Ingredients:

- 1 pack flour tortillas

- 1 cup shredded chicken breast or ground beef (cooked)

- 1 cup choice salsa

- 1/2 cup Cheddar cheese

- 1 cup shredded lettuce

- sour cream

- tomato sauce or tomato ketchup

Steps:

- Preheat oven to 350° F.

- Cut the tortillas into circles 4 inches in diameter, or big enough to fit in the muffin cups.

- Lay them flat in a plate and microwave for 15 minutes until softened.

- Grease the muffin tin.

- Press each tortilla into each cup while still warm and soft.

- Place a teaspoon of the Cheddar cheese in each tortilla cup.

- In a bowl, mix the meat and the salsa.

- Add a tablespoon of the mixture in the tortilla cups.

- Top each with another sprinkle of cheese.

- Bake for 20 minutes until the cheese melts and the tortillas turn crispy and brown at the edges.

- Serve with sour cream or more salsa and lettuce on top.

19. Homemade Meat Loaf Cups

Ingredients:

- 2 lb. lean ground beef

- 2 eggs

- 1 cup crispy bread crumbs

- 1 small red onion

- 2 cloves garlic (chopped)

- 1 tbsp. chopped Italian parsley

- 2 tsp. Worcestershire sauce

- 2/3 cup ketchup

- salt

- pepper

Steps:

- Preheat oven to 350° F.

- In a large bowl, mix all ingredients until well-combined.

- Grease the muffin tin or use cooking spray.

- Spoon the meat loaf mixture into each cup and press firmly.

- Bake for 35-40 minutes. Stick a meat thermometer at the center if a loaf. You may stop baking when it reaches 160° F.

- Let cool slightly before serving.

20. Cupcake Pizzas

Ingredients:

- Pillsbury Refrigerated Pizza Dough

- 1 cup pizza sauce or tomato sauce

- 3 cups shredded cheese

- sliced pepperoni

Steps:

- Preheat oven to 425° F.

- Lightly press and roll the dough to lengthen it a bit. Cut the dough into four parts. You can stretch it to six parts, but you have to make them thinner pizza muffins.

- Press each piece into the muffin tin cups. Cover the bottom and at least halfway up the sides.

- Pour a tablespoon of pizza sauce or tomato sauce over the dough.

- Sprinkle as much shredded cheese as you like over the sauce.

- Top with sliced pepperoni. As an alternative, you can also use sliced, cooked ham.

- Bake for 10-15 minutes.

21. Meatballs with Mashed Potato Garnish

Ingredients

- 1 lb. lean ground beef

- 1/2 lb. sweet Italian sausage

- 1 cup breadcrumbs

- 1 cup shredded carrots

- 1 cup pasta sauce

- 2 eggs

- 3 cups water

- 1 tsp. chopped garlic

- 1 tsp. chopped dried oregano leaves

- 1/2 cup chopped onions

- 1 tsp. pepper

- 1 tsp. salt

- 2 cups mashed potatoes (prepared beforehand and whipped with butter and milk)

- 1/2 bar cheese

Steps:

- Preheat oven to 450° F.

- In a large bowl, combine the beef and sausage, and add the breadcrumbs, carrots, pasta sauce, eggs, onions, garlic, oregano, cheddar cheese and half a cup of water. Season with half a teaspoon each of salt and pepper. Mix well.

- Cut the cheese into equal-sized 12 cubes.

- Scoop out the mixture and roll into 2 ½ inch balls.

- Insert the cheese into each ball and make sure it is entirely covered.

- Place one ball in each cup of the muffin tin. Bake for 20 minutes. Check that the meat is no longer pink.

- Top each meatball with a dollop of mashed potato and serve.

22. Barbecued Eggs in Muffin Tin

Ingredients:

- 12 eggs

- 1/3 cup chopped chives

- 1/2 cup chopped shallot

- 1/2 cup chopped red pepper

Steps:

- Preheat oven to 350° F.

- Generously spray cooking spray on the muffin tin.

- Crack an egg in each of the cups.

- Sprinkle a bit of the chives, shallot and pepper over each egg. You can add more seasoning if you wish.

- Bake for 5-10 minutes, depending on how cooked or runny you like the eggs to be

23. Sweet & Sour Meatloaves

Ingredients:

- 2 lbs. ground lean beef or sirloin

- 1 onion (chopped)

- 1 egg

- 1/4 cup brown sugar

- 1/2 cup crispy breadcrumbs

- 2 tbsps. vinegar

- 1 cup ketchup

- salt

- pepper

Steps:

- Preheat oven to 400° F.

- In a bowl, mix the brown sugar, vinegar and half cup of ketchup.

- Use cooking spray on the muffin tin.

- Scoop 2 1/2 teaspoons of the sauce in each cup.

- In another bowl, gently combine the ground meat with the onion, egg, bread crumbs and ½ cup ketchup.

- Form 12 meat balls and pop each in the muffin tin. Press and smoothen the surface of the meat.

- Bake for 20 minutes.

24. Kale Ricotta Cups

Ingredients:

- 4 cups chopped kale (stems excluded)

- 1 medium onion (diced)

- 2 garlic cloves (minced)

- 3 large eggs

- 1 cup sliced cherry tomatoes

- 450 grams ricotta cheese

- 1 tbsp. oregano

- 1/2 tsp. nutmeg

- salt

- pepper

Steps:

- Preheat oven to 375° F.

- Saute onions in olive oil for 5 minutes. Add garlic and kale, and stir until the latter wilts.

- In a bowl, beat the eggs, cheese, oregano, nutmeg, a bit of salt and pepper.

- Add the cooked kale and the cherry tomatoes.

- Grease muffin tin and spoon the mixture equally in each cup.

- Bake for 20 minutes.

25. Pan Potato Latkes

Ingredients:

- 2 cups shredded potatoes

- 1 1/2 cups shredded choice vegetables

- 1/2 cups oats

- 1 tbsp. canola oil

- 1 tsp. pepper

- 2 tsps. salt

Steps:

- Preheat oven to 400° F.

- Mix all ingredients in a large bowl.

- Grease the muffin tin.

- Scoop the mixture equally into each cup and bake for 20 minutes.

26. Sweet & Spicy Tuna Wonton Cups

Ingredients:

- 24 wonton skins

- 7 tbsps. olive oil

- 4 tbsps. sugar

- 3 tbsps. vinegar

- 2 tbsps. soy sauce

- 1/2 cup thinly sliced green onions

- 1/2 cup slivered almonds

- 2 cups shredded cabbage

- 2 Romain hearts (shredded)

- 1 can spicy tuna

- sesame seeds

Steps:

- Preheat oven to 350° F.

- Use cooking spray on the muffin tin.

- Place one or two wonton skins in each cup, covering the entire space.

- Bake for 10 minutes.

- Toast the almonds in one teaspoon olive oil.

- In a bowl, mix romaine, cabbage and onions.

- Drain the tuna and add to the salad. Mix well then spoon into the baked wonton cups.

- Sprinkle sesame seeds on top and serve.

27. Barbecue Beef Cups

Ingredients:

- 3/4 lb. ground beef

- 1/2 cup barbecue sauce

- 1 refrigerated biscuits dough

- 1 tbsp. brown sugar

- 3/4 cup cheddar cheese

Steps:

- Preheat oven to 400° F.

- Cook the beef over medium heat and remove the fatty oil.

- Remove from the stove and add barbecue sauce and brown sugar.

- Grease the muffin tin.

- Cut up the dough into pieces big enough to line the inside of each cup, up to the sides.

- Spoon the beef mixture equally into each cup.

- Sprinkle cheese on top and bake for 10-12 minutes.

28. Mini Fritatas

Ingredients:

- 1 medium zucchini (sliced)
- 1 red bell pepper (sliced)
- 1 yellow bell pepper (sliced)
- 4 white mushrooms
- 16 eggs
- 1 tbsp. chopped chives
- 2 tsps. salt
- 3/4 tsps. ground black pepper
- 1/2 cup grated cheese

Steps:

- Preheat oven to 400° F.
- In a bowl, whisk the eggs, chives, salt and pepper.
- Grease the muffin tin and place some of the zucchini and peppers in each cup.
- Pour egg mixture in each cup up near the rim.

- Sprinkle with cheese and bake for 10 minutes.

Chapter 6: Muffin Tin Recipes For Dinner

Dinner is a leisurely affair. We enjoy delicious, sumptuous dishes that are meant to be savored and enjoyed without any hurry. What's great about dinner is you can have a light one or go for a more filling dish.

29. Mini Chicken Pot Pies

Ingredients:

- 1lb boneless chicken breasts

- 1/2 cup chicken broth

- 1 medium onion (chopped)

- 1 cup mix of frozen peas and carrots

- 1 tbsp. vegetable oil

- 1 cup Cheddar cheese (shredded)

- 1/4 tsp. pepper

- 1/4 tsp. salt

- 1/4 tsp. ground thyme

- 2 eggs

- 1/2 cup milk

- 1/2 cup Original Bisquick mix

Steps:

- Cut chicken into bite-sized pieces.

- Preheat oven at 375° F.

- Pour the oil in a skillet and stir-cook the chicken over medium heat for 5-7 minutes.

- Add onion and chicken broth, and let it simmer.

- Add the frozen vegetables and season to taste. Stir until most of the broth is absorbed.

- Let cool before stirring in the cheese.

- In another bowl, mix the eggs, milk and Original Bisquick mix with a whisk.

- Take a muffin pan and lightly flatten 1 tablespoon of the mixture in each cup. Top with a bit of the chicken mixture, then cover with another layer of the Bisquick mix.

- Bake for 25-30 minutes. Serve warm.

30. Spicy Chicken Cakes

Ingredients:

- 3 large, chicken thighs, boneless(finely diced)

- 8 ounces cream cheese (keep at room temperature)

- 8 ounces blue cheese (crumbled)

- 1 cup Saucy Mama sauce for hot wings

- 4 celery sticks (diced)

- 1 1/2 cups Parmesan cheese

- 1 cup melted butter

- 3 cups panko

- 4 tbsp. chopped chives

Steps:

- Preheat oven at 350° F.

- Toss together the diced chicken meat, cream cheese, hot sauce, and half of the blue cheese in a large bowl.

- In another bowl, mix the panko and the remaining half of the Parmesan. Add the chives and melted butter. Toss with a fork until the dry ingredients are moistened.

31. Chinese Takeout in Muffin Cups

Ingredients:

- 1 lb. uncooked shrimp, peeled

- 1 bag Green Giant Steamers frozen rice & vegetables

- 1 can Pillsbury refrigerated crescent dinner rolls

- 1 cup shredded toasted coconut

- 1 cup diced pineapple

- 1 tbsp. soy sauce

- 1 tbsp. olive oil

- 1/2 tsp. salt

- 1/2 tsp. garam masala

- 2 tbsps. chopped cilantro

- pepper

Steps:

- Preheat oven at 400° F.

- Unroll the Pillsbury dinner roll dough and press the surface to seal any breaks.

- Sprinkle coconut over one side of the roll and gently press the grains to the dough.

- Cut dough into eight parts. Each should fit in your muffin tin.

- Press a piece of dough in each cup, coconut-sprinkled side down.

- Bake for 10 minutes until golden brown.

- Right after baking, use the bottom of a slim glass or marble pestle to press the dough inside the cup to assume the shape.

- Season the shrimp with salt, masala and pepper.

- In a wide pan, heat the olive oil over medium heat then add the shrimp. Stir constantly until they turn pink.

- Add the frozen rice & vegetables, pineapple and soy sauce. Stir until thoroughly cooked.

- Scoop the shrimp and rice into the baked cups. Top with cilantro and serve.

32. Mini Lasagna

Ingredients:

- 12 oz. ground turkey

- 15 oz. tomato sauce (usually 1 can's worth)

- 24 wonton wrappers

- 1 medium onion (chopped)

- 1/2 cup chopped mushrooms

- 1/4 tsp. pepper

- 1/4 tsp. salt

- 2 garlic cloves (chopped)

- 1 1/2 cups ricotta cheese

- 1 1/2 cups mozzarella cheese

- 1 1/2 tsps. chopped oregano

- 1/2 tsp. chopped basil

Steps:

- Preheat oven at 375° F.

- Over medium heat, cook the ground turkey, onions, and season with salt and pepper. Stir until the turkey meat turns brown.

- Add the garlic and cook for another minute.

- Add tomato sauce and one teaspoon of oregano.

- Let the sauce boil gently and let simmer for 10 minutes, then set aside.

- In a bowl, mix the ricotta cheese, the remaining oregano, basil, and some salt and pepper.

- Generously grease the muffin tin.

- Press one wonton wrapper in each cup.

- Use half of the ricotta mixture and pour it evenly in each cup.

- Use half of the turkey and tomato sauce as well, and pour them evenly in each cup.

- Sprinkle mozzarella cheese.

- Press another wonton wrapper on top and then work on a second layer.

- Bake for 10 minutes until the cheese on top melts. Sprinkle with basil and serve.

33. Mac & Cheese

Ingredients:

- 1 cup elbow macaroni

- 3 cups finely crushed cereal

- 2 1/2 cups Cheddar cheese

- 1 cup warmed whole milk

- 1 egg (separate the yolk and egg white)

- 1 tbsp. flour blend

- 5 tbsps. unsalted melted butter

- 1/4 tsp. salt

Steps:

- Cook the macaroni as directed, then drain.

- Preheat oven at 350° F.

- In a bowl, mix the cereal with four tablespoons melted butter and a cup of the shredded cheese.

- Grease the muffin tin.

- Divide evenly among the cups and press firmly along the bottom and sides.

- Heat the remaining butter and flour blend in a saucepan for a minute. Slowly add the warmed milk and whisk for a few minutes until thickened.

- Remove the pan from the stove and add another cup of cheese. Stir until melted.

- Add in the macaroni, salt and egg yolk.

- Beat the egg white until you have thick foam. Pour in the macaroni mixture and fold.

- Spoon into the prepared cups and top with the remaining cheese.

- Bake for 20 minutes.

34. Caramelized Onion Potato Cakes

Ingredients:

- 1 large sweet onion (sliced)

- 8 oz. ready to cook mashed potatoes

- 3 cups milk

- 3 cups water

- 7 tbsps. butter

- 1/3 cup crumbled Gorgonzola cheese

- 1/8 tsp. salt

Steps:

- Preheat oven at 375° F. Place foil liners in the muffin tin.

- In a non-stick pan, melt one tablespoon butter over medium heat. Add onions and stir for 10 minutes, making sure they are well-coated in butter. Season with salt and stir until onions are golden brown.

- In a saucepan, heat water, milk and butter until boiling. Remove from stove.

- Add mashed potatoes and stir until blended.

- Add cheese and thyme, and stir again. If it's still runny, let it sit for a moment and let the potatoes absorb the moisture

- Spoon three tablespoons of the mixture in each muffin cup.

- Top each cup with one tablespoon onions.

- Scoop the remaining mashed potatoes in a plastic bag and pipe them on top like icing.

- Bake for 10-15 minutes.

35. Ricotta Spinach Cups

Ingredients:

- 24 wonton wrappers

- 1 cup ricotta cheese

- 10 oz. chopped spinach

- 2 eggs

- 1 garlic clove (chopped)

- 1 tbsp. cream

- 1/4 cup grated parmesan cheese

- 1/4 tsp. pepper

- 1/4 tsp. salt

- 1/8 tsp. grated nutmeg

Steps:

- Preheat oven at 350° F.

- Lightly spray cooking spray on the muffin tin.

- Press one wonton wrapper in each cup and spray the top again.

- Bake for 5 minutes. Remove when done then do the same to the second batch.

- In a bowl, combine the cheese, spinach, eggs, garlic, spices and nuts.

- Fill the baked wonton cups with a teaspoon of the mixture and pop back in the muffin tin. Bake for 15 minutes. Repeat for the next batch.

36. Pork Loin & Shrimp Wontons

Ingredients:

- 24 wonton wrappers

- 1/2 lb. ground pork loin

- 3 oz. finely chopped shrimp

- 1 oz. sliced dried ear mushrooms

- 1/4 tsp. white pepper

- 1/2 tsp. salt

- 1 tsp. chopped ginger

- 1 tbsp. corn starch

- 2 tbsps. chopped green onions

Steps:

- Preheat oven at 350° F.

- In a bowl, mix well the pork, shrimp, mushrooms, spices and cornstarch.

- Grease the muffin tin.

- Arrange and press two wonton wrappers in each cup.

- Place one teaspoon of the mixture in each cup. Sprinkle the chopped green onions on top.

- Bake for 10-15 minutes.

37. Goat Cheese Fritatas

Ingredients:

- 1 tbsp. unsalted butter

- 2 tbsps. milk

- 2 tsps. kosher salt

- 1 medium yellow onion (diced)

- 2 tbsps. olive oil

- 9 large eggs

- 8 oz. cremini mushrooms (sliced)

- 4 oz. crumbled goat cheese

- 1/2 tsp. chopped thyme

- ground black pepper

Steps:

- Preheat oven at 350° F.

- In a skillet, melt butter with a tablespoon of olive oil. Add onions until golden. Season with salt and pepper, then add thyme. Pour in a bowl and set aside.

- In another pan, heat to simmer the remaining olive oil then add the mushrooms. Season with salt and pepper, and continue to stir until cooked.

- Add the mushrooms to the cooked onions.

- Add goat cheese and mix well.

- Grease the muffin tin.

- Place a heaping tablespoon of the mixture in each cup.

- In another bowl, whisk the eggs and add milk and a little salt.

- Pour the egg mixture to each cup until almost full.

- Bake for 12-15 minutes.

38. Chicken Alfredo Pies

Ingredients:

- 2 cups chopped cooked chicken

- 1 cup uncooked penne pasta

- 15 oz. pasta Alfredo sauce

- 1 roll biscuit dough

- 9 oz. frozen spinach (thawed and drained)

- 1/2 cup shredded parmesan

Steps:

- Preheat oven at 360° F.

- Cook pasta as instructed, drain and place in a mixing bowl.

- Add the cooked chicken, Alfredo sauce and spinach.

- Cut the dough into eight equal parts.

- Grease the muffin tin.

- Press a piece of dough in each cup, up to the sides.

- Add a spoon of the chicken mix in each cup and sprinkle with cheese.

- Bake for 20 minutes.

39. Mini Shepherd's Pie

Ingredients:

- 12 Pillsbury Grands! Refrigerated buttermilk biscuits dough

- 1 lb. ground beef

- 2 tbsps. olive oil

- 1/2 cup beef stock

- 1 cup frozen mixed vegetables

- 1 1/2 cups mashed potatoes

- 2 cups cheddar cheese

- 1/2 onion (sliced)

- 1 1/2 tsps. salt

- 1 tbsp. minced garlic

- 1 tbsp. ground pepper

- 2 tbsps. all-purpose flour

- 2 tbsps. chopped parsley leaves

- 1 tbsp. chopped rosemary leaves

- 1 tbsp. garlic powder

- 2 tbsps. onion powder

Steps:

- Preheat oven at 425° F.

- Grease the muffin tin.

- Press a biscuit dough in each cup up to the sides and bake for 5 minutes.

- In a skillet, cook the ground beef in olive oil. Add onions, salt, garlic and pepper.

- Slowly mix the oil until the meat mixture turns pasty.

- Add the beef stock, vegetables and herbs. Mix well.

- In another pan, reheat the mash and season with garlic and onion powder.

- Add two tablespoons of mash in each cup. Spoon in another two tablespoons of beef and sprinkle with cheddar cheese.

- Bake for 15 minutes.

40. Tomato Hand Pies

Ingredients:

- 6 small tomatoes

- 8 oz. sweet Italian sausage (crumbled)

- 1 sheet puff pastry dough (10 x 10 inches)

- 1 small onion (chopped)

- 1 small celery stalk (half-moon cuts)

- 1 tbsp. heavy cream

- 1 tbsp. olive oil

- 2 tbsps. finely chopped parsley

- 1/2 cup grated parmesan cheese

- 1 egg

- Salt

Steps:

- Preheat oven at 400° F.

- Cut off the tops of the tomatoes and set aside. Clean the insides, salt the inner skin and place upside down on a rack to drain.

- Grease the muffin tin.

- Cut dough into six parts and press each in the cups (allow overhangs).

- Pop in the tomato skins and slightly turn up the dough to encase the tomato fully.

- In a skillet, heat olive oil then add onions and celery. Cook for three minutes, then add the sausage. Stir until cooked. Remove from the stove and add the parsley and cheese.

- Spoon the mixture inside the tomato skins/shells.

- Beat the egg and cream, and brush on the overhanging dough.

- Bake for 15 minutes.

41. Philly Cheesesteak Bites

Ingredients:

- 2 lbs. ground sirloin

- 1 chopped small yellow onion

- 1 chopped red bell pepper

- 1 chopped green bell pepper

- 1/4 cup Worcestershire sauce

- 1/2 cup milk

- 1 1/2 cups pancake mix

- 2 cups shredded cheese

- salt

- pepper

Steps:

- Preheat oven at 400° F. Place the muffin tins for a few minutes to heat them.

- Cook the meat in a pan over medium heat until brown. Add the onions, pepper and Worcestershire sauce. Let cool.

- In a bowl, pour the pancake mix, milk, cooked meat, salt, pepper, and 1 1/2 cups cheese.

- Use cooking spray on the muffin tin.

- Evenly scoop the mixture into the cups. Sprinkle the remaining cheese on top.

- Bake for 15 minutes.

42. Broccoli Quiches

Ingredients:

- 10 oz. frozen broccoli (thawed and drained)

- 4 eggs

- 1 cup milk

- 1 tbsp. baking powder

- 1 cup cheddar cheese

- 1/2 cup flour

- 1/2 cup diced onions

- 1/2 tsp. salt

- 1/4 tsp. pepper

Steps:

- Preheat oven at 400° F.

- In a bowl, beat the eggs with milk.

- Add baking powder, flour, frozen broccoli, cheddar cheese and onions. Mix well. Season with salt and pepper.

- Grease the muffin tin.

- Spoon the mixture into the cups and bake for 20 minut

Chapter 7: Best Muffin Tin Recipes For After School Snacks

Give your kids something yummy to look forward to after school! Reward their hard work in studying and other activities with these delicious after-school snacks.

43. Cheeseburger Muffin

Ingredients:

- 1 lb. ground beef

- 1 cup chopped onions

- 1 cup Cheddar cheese

- 1/2 tsp. salt

- 1/2 cup Original Bisquick Mix

- 2 eggs

- 1 cup milk

Steps:

- Preheat oven to 400° F.

- Using a skillet, cook the beef and onion together for up to 10 minutes over medium heat. Stop when the beef has turned brown, then drain.

- Season with salt.

- Spritz the muffin tin with cooking spray or use a non-stick muffin baking tin.

- Spoon the beef into each cup, filling about 3/4 of it. Don't flatten, just leave it loosely in.

- Sprinkle Cheddar cheese onto the beef.

- In another bowl, whisk the eggs, milk and Bisquick mix until well blended.

- Pour a bit of the mix into each cup until almost filled.

- Place the muffin tin in the oven and bake for 25 minutes. Best served warm.

44. Donut Muffins

Ingredients:

- 3/4 cup all-purpose flour. Have an extra 1 tbsp. on hand.

- 1/4 cup whole wheat pastry flour

- 1 tsp. baking powder

- 1/2 cup fine or confectioner's sugar

- 2 tbsp. unsalted butter (alternative: vegetable shortening)

- 1/2 tsp. salt

- 1/2 tsp. grated nutmeg

- 1/4 cup plain or choice flavor yogurt

- 1/4 cup whole cream milk

- 1 egg

- 1 tsp. vanilla extract

- 1/2 cup chocolate chips (you may have both white and milk chocolate, depending on your preference)

Steps:

- Preheat oven to 350° F.

- In a large bowl, sift together the flours and baking powder.

- Add the sugar, salt and nutmeg. Whisk to mix.

- Add in the butter or vegetable shortening. Using your fingers, mix the ingredients together until the dry ingredients are moistened and resembles pastry crust.

- Pour the yogurt, milk, egg and vanilla extract. Fold until combined, but do not overmix the dough.

- Grease the muffin tin or spritz with cooking spray.

- Spoon in the dough until three-quarters of the cups are full. Another option is to pour the dough in a piping bag, use it to fill the muffin cups and leave a space in the middle to make it donut-like. Either will be fine.

- Bake for 10 minutes or until the donut muffins spring back to form when touched.

- Melt the chocolate chips in a bowl held over boiled water. Use to glaze the donut muffins. Add sprinkles or confectioner's sugar, as desired.

45. Frozen Smoothie Cups

Ingredients:

- 3 cups strongly brewed coffee (allow to cool)

- 2 bananas

- 1 tsp. cinnamon

- 2 tsp. vanilla extract

- 1/2 cup chocolate powder or protein mix

- 1/2 cup chopped dried dates

- 1/2 cup almonds or pecans

- blender

Steps:

- Pour the coffee in the blender. Add the bananas, chocolate powder or chocolate protein mix, dried dates and nuts.

- Blend on low setting or manually process for a few moments first before using the higher setting. Blend until the dry ingredients are thoroughly grinded and you end up with a smooth consistency.

- Take a muffin tin and pour the smoothie mixture into the cups.

- Put in the freezer overnight or until the smoothie cups harden.

- To extract the frozen cups, fill a large, flat tray with water. Dip the bottom of the muffin tray in the water. Grip the opposite sides of the tray and gently twist to dislodge the frozen smoothing cups.

46. Apple Pie Muffins

Ingredients:

- 1 cup pancake mix

- 1/4 cup packed brown sugar

- 1/2 cup granulated sugar

- 1/4 cup chopped nuts

- 3 tbsps. butter

- 3 cups sliced apples (already peeled)

- 2 eggs

- 1 tsp. cinnamon powder

- 1/4 tsp. ground nutmeg

- 1/2 cup milk

Steps:

- Preheat oven to 325° F.

- Place the apple slices in a bowl. Add the cinnamon powder and nutmeg and toss.

- Grease the muffin tin.

- Using a fork, scoop the apples into each cup.

- In a bigger bowl, mix the milk, eggs, granulated sugar, a tablespoon of butter and half the cup of pancake mix.

- Pour this mix into each cup of the muffin tin, right over the apples.

- In another bowl, mix half of the pancake mix with the chopped nuts, packed brown sugar, and two tablespoons of the butter until you get a crumbly mixture.

- Sprinkle over each cup.

- Bake from 40-45 minutes.

- May be served with a scoop of ice cream on top.

47. Snickers Cheesecake

Ingredients:

- 3 Snickers bars (chopped)

- 2 cups crushed graham crackers (18 pcs. graham crackers)

- 8 ounces cream cheese

- 2 eggs

- 5 tbsps. melted butter

- 1 tbsp. vanilla extract

- 1 cup granulated sugar

- 1/4 cup caramel sauce

- whipped cream

Steps:

- Preheat oven to 350° F.

- Combine crushed grahams, melted butter and two tablespoons of sugar in a bowl until well-mixed.

- Place muffin liners in the muffin tin.

- Scoop two tablespoons of the mixture into each cup. Press it to the bottom and up the sides of the cup (as high as you can) using your thumbs.

- Bake for six minutes until the crust turns brown.

- In a bowl, combine the cream cheese and sugar and beat with a mixer until creamy.

- While mixing, add the eggs one at a time, then vanilla, and lastly the caramel sauce.

- Scoop the cream cheese mixture into the muffin tin. Don't fill the cups to the brim, though.

- Top with crushed Snickers bars.

- Bake for 25 minutes until the edges turn slightly brown.

- Let cool completely before serving. Drizzle with extra caramel sauce and top with whipped cream.

48. Mini Corn Dogs

- Ingredients:

- 10 beef hotdogs

- 1 cup all-purpose flour

- 1 cup cornmeal

- 1 cup buttermilk

- 2 eggs

- 1/2 cup melted butter

- 1/2 cup sugar

- 1/2 tbsp. baking soda

- 1/2 tsp. salt

Steps:

- Cut the hotdogs into 1-inch slices.

- Preheat oven to 375° F.

- In a bowl, whisk butter and sugar together. Add the eggs and then buttermilk. Whisk until well-blended.

- In another bowl, mix the flour, cornmeal, baking soda and salt.

- Slowly add and whisk into the first bowl.

- Grease a muffin tin.

- Place a tablespoon of the batter into each cup, then stick a hotdog at centers.

- Bake for 8-12 minutes until the cornbread turns brown.

49. Soup Cups

Ingredients:

- leftover soup or the ingredients to your favorite soup
- plastic wrap

Steps:

- Pour the leftover soup in a baking tin without overflowing each cup.
- An alternative is to cook a fresh batch of your favorite soup. Let cool before pouring in the muffin tin.
- Cover completely with a plastic wrap.
- Keep in freezer. Should you wish to have soup, just pop one or two frozen cups and heat in a pan.

50. Mini Deep Pizzas

Ingredients:

- 1 pack wonton skins
- 1 lb. lean ground beef
- 2 cups mozzarella cheese
- 1 cup chopped tomato

- 1 jar pizza or tomato sauce

- pepperoni or ham slices (or bits)

Steps:

- Preheat oven to 400° F.

- Cut up the pizza dough into six equal sizes.

- In a pan, cook the beef and season to taste. Add the pizza/tomato sauce.

- Grease the muffin tin.

- Place one wonton skin in each cup. If they are too small, you can overlap two or three skins.

- Spoon the beef into each cup. Top with cheese and pepperoni or ham.

- You can add another layer if your muffin tin is deep.

- Bake for about 15 minutes or until the cheese melts.

51. Spaghetti Nests

Ingredients:

- 10 ounces dry wheat spaghetti

- 1 cup cottage cheese

- 1/2 cup cheddar cheese

- 1/4 tsp. pepper

- 1/4 tsp. smoked paprika

- 1 tsp. turmeric powder

- 1/2 cup shredded parmesan cheese

- olive oil

Steps:

- Cook spaghetti as instructed. Don't break the noodles, and keep half of the liquid afterwards.

- Preheat oven to 425° F.

- In a bowl, combine cottage and cheddar cheese.

- Toss in the spaghetti noodles. Add olive oil and spices.

- Lightly use cooking spray on the muffin tin.

- Using a fork, twirl a portion of the spaghetti until you have a "nest" that will fit into the muffin cups. Fill all cups and top with parmesan cheese.

- Bake for 10 minutes until the tops cheese has melted and the tops are semi-brown.

52. Pumpkin Cheesecake

Ingredients:

- 8 oz. cream cheese

- 20 pcs. gingersnap cookies

- 2 tbsps. melted butter

- 1/2 cup canned pumpkin

- 1/2 cup packed brown sugar

- 1 tbsp. sour cream (alternative: lemon zest)

- 1 egg

- 1 tsp. vanilla

- 1/4 tsp. salt

- 1/2 tsp. ground cinnamon

- 1/4 tsp. grated nutmeg

- whipped cream

- caramel sauce

Steps:

- Preheat oven to 350° F.

- Use a food processor or blender to grind the cookies. Add butter and grind to form the crust.

- Spray the muffin tray.

- Scoop the crust evenly into each cup and press at the bottom and sides.

- Bake for 8 minutes.

- Using a mixer, beat the cream cheese and add the brown sugar until fluffy. Add the pumpkin, sour cream or lemon zest and salt. Beat.

- Add egg, vanilla, cinnamon and nutmeg, and beat again.

- Spoon the mixture evenly into the crust cups.

- Bake for 20-25 minutes.

- Let cool completely and refrigerate overnight before serving.

53. Cookies & Cream Cheesecake

Ingredients:

- 20 pcs. Oreo vanilla cookies

- 2 tbsps. melted butter

- 8 oz. cream cheese

- 1 egg

- 1 tsp. shortening

- 2 tbsps. sugar

- 3 tbsps. chocolate chips

- 1/4 cup milk

Steps:

- Preheat oven to 325° F.

- Place cupcake liners in the muffin tin.

- Place 16 pieces of the Oreo cookies and crush with a rolling pin. Pour in a bowl and add melted butter. Mix well.

- Press one teaspoon of the mixture firmly at the bottom of the cups.

- Using a mixer, beat together the cream cheese, sugar and milk until fluffy. Add egg and vanilla, and beat again.

- Break each of the remaining four cookies into chunks. Add and fold into the cream cheese.

- Spoon mixture into each cup.

- Bake for 15 minutes.

- Let cool and refrigerate before serving. Serve with chocolate chips as garnish. You can also melt them and drizzle on top.

54. Triple Berry Cheesecakes

Ingredients:

- 8 oz. cream cheese

- 12 oz. fresh strawberry yogurt

- 1 egg

- 1/3 cup sugar

- 2 tsps. cornstarch

- 1 1/2 cups crushed cereal or graham crackers

- 2 tbsps. sugar

- 2 tbsps. melted butter

- 2 cups freshly sliced berries and raspberries

- 1/4 cup chocolate chips

Steps:

- Preheat oven 300° F.

- Place cupcake liners in the muffin tin.

- Mix well the crushed cereal or grahams, sugar and margarine in a bowl.

- Press one teaspoon of the mixture firmly at the bottom of the cups.

- Beat the cream cheese, sugar and egg until fluffy. Add yogurt and cornstarch, and continue beating until blended.

- Spoon mixture into each cup.

- Bake for 20 minutes until the sides turn firm. Let cool and refrigerate.

Top each cheesecake cup with fresh berries and chocolate chips. You may also melt the chocolate and drizzle them instead.

55. Kiwi-Lime Dessert Cups

Ingredients:

- 1 pack refrigerated cookie dough

- 1 lime

- 2 oz. cream cheese

- 2 tbsp. confectioner's sugar

- 1/2 cup sliced toasted almonds

- green food coloring

- 2 cups frozen whipped topping

- strawberries

- kiwi

Steps:

- Preheat oven to 350° F.

- Cut the cookie dough roll into six disks, 1/2 inch thick.

- Set aside two tablespoons of the almonds. Grind the rest in a food processor, then dip the six pieces of dough until well-coated.

- Grease the muffin tin.

- Cut each disk into four and place each smaller piece in the muffin tray cups.

- Bake for 11 minutes. The dough by then will expand and take the shape of the cup. Let cool then remove the baked cups.

- Zest one tablespoon off the lemon and squeeze out one tablespoon of juice.

- In a bowl, combine the cream cheese, lemon zest and juice, sugar and food coloring. Whisk until smooth, then add whipped topping and fold. Pour the mixture in a piping bag or plastic bag.

- Pipe the cream on top of each of the baked cups.

- Slice the strawberries and kiwi thinly. Stick one slice of each on top of the cream, along with the remaining almonds.

Chapter 8: Muffin Tin Cooking Tips

Keep in mind the following tips so that you can achieve perfect muffin tin dishes each time:

- Be familiar with the quirks of your oven. There are some ovens whose actual temperatures are different from what the dial or screen says. If your oven at home is the same, adjust the temperatures of the recipes you are following accordingly.

- Use cooking spray so that it will be easy to pop out the muffins without destroying the shape of the cup.

- For the cheesecake recipes, always use cupcake liners.

- When using cream cheese, make sure it is softened an in room temperature first before beating. This prevents the cream cheese muffin to break or crack after baking.

- If you are using a 12-cup muffin pan and the recipe doesn't seem to be enough to fill all cups, leave a cup empty at intervals. Fill them with ¾ water to prevent the metal from warping due to heat.

- Place a baking sheet between the muffin tin and the rack in the oven. This helps make it easier to slide the muffin tin in and out of the oven.

- If you find it difficult to pop a muffin off the cup, get a towel and wet it with lukewarm water. Spread it on a flat surface and place the hot muffin tin on top for a few minutes. Then you can try again and extract the muffin.

Chapter 9: Mistakes To Avoid

Before performing the recipes above, review these common mistakes and keep in mind how you can avoid them.

- A lot is riding on the quality of the equipment and materials used for cooking and baking. Since the primary accessory needed for the recipes above is a muffin tin, consider quality when buying one. Avoid using muffin tins that are affordable but too thin as they might cause the food to burn.

- Filling a muffin cup to the brim when the recipe includes baking powder or baking soda. This results in flat muffins, because there is no room for the dough to rise and expand.

- Baking a second batch of the same recipe without washing the muffin tin. Some people think that since it's basically the same dish, it will be fine not to wash the tin anymore when baking a second round. This is wrong. The food particles left in the tin will burn during its second round in the oven, and thus affecting both the taste and shape of the second batch. The burnt particles are likely to stick to the tin, making it difficult to pop the new muffin off the cup.

- Frequently opening the oven to check on the baking muffin meals. If your oven doesn't have a clear glass door, resist the temptation to constantly open and check on what's going on inside. The heat will escape and affect the temperature inside the oven.

-   Not using measuring tools for the ingredients. Unless if you're an expert baker or cook and you can accurately estimate quantities without using a measuring cup or spoon, make use of the tools in your kitchen.

-   Switching ingredients for another without considering their purpose in the recipe. If you don't have baking powder, remember that it can't be replaced by baking soda. If you want to make a gluten-free dessert, best research for a different recipe altogether instead of leaving out the oats, bread crumbs altogether.

Chapter 10: Suitable Special Occasions For Muffin Tin Recipes

These recipes are great because they are relatively easy to do, and can be done in under an hour. What's more, these are dishes and snacks that you can serve whenever you have company, or when you are attending a celebration.

Muffin tin meals are basically finger foods, only they are more filling. The fact that they are compact makes them the ideal type of food to serve in parties where guests are expected to stand a lot and mingle with one another. Examples of such occasions are:

- Barbecue parties
- Outdoor company events
- Cocktail parties (or when serving cocktails in a day-long celebration)
- House parties
- Birthdays
- Weddings
- Bridal showers
- Baby showers
- Fourth of July
- Christmas Parties
- Reunions
- Product launchings
- Semi-formal gatherings
- Casual gatherings
- Potluck neighborhood parties

... or in any other event where it is more convenient to hold a small plate of food while socializing with other people, as opposed to finding a place to sit down and actually use a spoon and fork while eating. With these dishes, a dessert fork will be sufficient to eat.

Conclusion

Thank you again for purchasing the book ***Muffin Tin Recipes: Mouthwatering Muffin Tin Recipes in 20 minutes***!

I am extremely excited to pass this information along to you, and I am so happy that you now have read and can hopefully implement these strategies going forward.

I hope this book was able to help learn new simple recipes and how to bake delicious, single-portion meals.

The next step is to get started using this information and to hopefully be more active in the kitchen from now on!

Please don't be someone who just reads this information and doesn't apply it, the strategies in this book will only benefit you if you use them!

If you know of anyone else that could benefit from the information presented here please inform them of this book.

Finally, if you enjoyed this book and feel it has added value to your life in any way, please take the time to share your thoughts and post a review on Amazon. It'd be greatly appreciated!

Thank you and good luck!

Preview Of:
The Clean Eating Ultimate Cookbook And Diet Guide!

<u>Clean Eating</u>

Low Fat, Paleo, And Low Carb Recipes For Maximum Weight Loss And To Boost Your Metabolism For Fast Results!

Introduction

I want to thank you and congratulate you for purchasing the book, "Clean Eating: The Clean Eating Ultimate Cookbook and Diet Guide! – Low Fat, Paleo, And Low Carb Recipes For Maximum Weight Loss And To Boost Your Metabolism for Fast Results!"

This book contains proven steps and strategies on how to lose weight and boost your metabolism as quickly as possible based on the principles of clean eating and using popular diet recipes like low fat, paleo, and low carb recipes.

These days, you need to be more mindful of the kinds of food that you eat. You have to make sure that what you are eating is as natural as possible to provide you with the essential nutrients that your body needs without worrying about side effects or acquiring diseases. People these days choose convenience over health by buying processed and ready-to-eat foods that` do not contribute much to your health. In this fast paced world where fast food and instant meals are popular, you have to be more disciplined with the meals that you cook not only for yourself but also for your whole family.

This book will give you some basic facts and background on the principles of clean eating and different kinds of diet plans and strategies like low fat, paleo, low carb, carb cycling, flexible, and IIFYM. You can also find some tips on how to lose maximum weight, boost your metabolism, and get in shape. To get you started on your clean eating diet plan, you can use the recipes provided in the last few chapters of this book.

Thanks again for purchasing this book, I hope you enjoy it!

Chapter 1: Clean Eating Cookbook And Diet Guide

You have probably heard of clean eating from one of your health conscious or diet enthusiast friends. If not, you are probably asking the question that many people are asking, what exactly is clean eating? The main concept of clean eating is eating foods at their most natural state. This includes foods that are raw, fresh, and unprocessed. It is not just about the quantity but more on the quality of food that you eat. Clean eating is not just a diet fad or trend. It is a sound approach to healthy living through eating the right kinds of food that gives you the energy you need and makes you a healthier individual.

If you are going to adopt clean eating in your lifestyle, you need to understand its basic principles.

Eat whole and natural foods

Whole and natural foods are foods that have not been processed and are usually packed in a box, can, and plastic packaging. A bag of fresh beans may be packed in a plastic bag but this does not mean that these beans are not whole or natural. It is important that the foods that you eat are fresh or are in their most natural state, which means less cooking and very little processing, if at all.

Add fat, carbohydrate, and protein to your diet

Good fat and carbohydrate are essential minerals and they are easy to get from the usual foods that you eat everyday like grains, oil, pasta, and so on. However, many people lack protein in their diet, especially breakfast. It is important to get the right amount of protein that your body needs to help develop your muscles and also make you feel full longer.

Eat small meals frequently

The clean eating diet advises you to eat about five to six small meals in a day. This includes the usual breakfast, lunch, and dinner, plus two to three snacks in between meals. By eating small meals frequently, you will not go hungry easily which can often lead to overeating or eating just about anything you can grab. The small meals throughout the day also help stabilize the level of sugar in your bloodstream which prevents energy lag.

Drink at least two liters of water per day

This will keep your body hydrated which will prevent you from feeling tired. Avoid high calorie drinks like soda or energy drink because you need to get your calories from the food that you eat and not your drinks. It is also important to use a reusable canteen rather than plastic.

Learn how to read labels

Clean eating requires you to learn how to read labels because this is where you will find the ingredients. If the list of ingredients contain long names that are difficult to pronounce, this could mean that it has an artificial ingredient which is banned from clean eating.

Thanks for Previewing My Exciting Book Entitled:

"Clean Eating: The Clean Eating Ultimate Cookbook And Diet Guide! Low Fat, Paleo, And Low Carb Recipes For Maximum Weight Loss And To Boost Your Metabolism For Fast Results!"

To purchase this book, simply go to the Amazon Kindle store and simply search:

"CLEAN EATING"

Then just scroll down until you see my book. You will know it is mine because you will see my name "Sarah Brooks" underneath the title.

Alternatively, you can visit my author page on Amazon to see this book and other work I have done. Thanks so much, and please don't forget your free bonuses

DON'T LEAVE YET! - CHECK OUT YOUR FREE BONUSES BELOW!

Free Bonus Offer: Get Free Access To The www.LuxyLifeNaturals.com VIP Newsletter!

Once you enter your email address you will immediately get free access to this awesome newsletter!

But wait, right now if you join now for free you will also get free access to the "Anti-Aging Made Easy" free EBook!

To claim both your FREE VIP NEWSLETTER MEMBERSHIP and your FREE BONUS Ebook on ANTI-AGING MADE EASY!

Just Go To:

www.LuxyLifeNaturals.com

Manufactured by Amazon.ca
Bolton, ON

18663035R00055